Bats

by Bibi Boynton

Reading Consultant: Wiley Blevins, M.A.
Phonics/Early Reading Specialist

 COMPASS POINT BOOKS

Minneapolis, Minnesota

Compass Point Books
A Capstone Imprint
1710 Roe Crest Drive
North Mankato, MN 56003

Visit Compass Point Books on the Internet at *www.capstonepub.com*

Editorial Development: Alice Dickstein, Alice Boynton
Photo Researcher: Wanda Winch
Design/Page Production: Silver Editions, Inc.

Library of Congress Cataloging-in-Publication Data
Boynton, Bibi.
 Bats / by Bibi Boynton.
     p. cm. — (Compass Point phonics readers)
 Summary: Briefly introduces the physical characteristics and behavior of
 bats, in a text that incorporates phonics instruction.
 Includes bibliographical references and index.
  ISBN-10: 0-7565-0505-4 (hardcover : alk. paper)
  ISBN-13: 978-0-7565-0505-9 (hardcover : alk. paper)
  1. Bats—Juvenile literature. 2. Reading—Phonetic method—Juvenile
 literature. [1. Bats. 2. Reading—Phonetic method.] I. Title. II. Series.
 QL737.C5B5727 2003
 599.4--dc21   2003006349

Printed in the United States of America in North Mankato, Minnesota.
042012   006527R

Table of Contents

Dear Parent or Caregiver,

Welcome to Compass Point Phonics Readers, books of information for young children. Each book concentrates on specific phonic sounds and words commonly found in beginning reading materials. Featuring eye-catching photographs, every book explores a single science or social studies concept that is sure to grab a child's interest.

So snuggle up with your child, and let's begin. Start by reading aloud the Mother Goose nursery rhyme on the next page. As you read, stress the words in dark type. These are the words that contain the phonic sounds featured in this book. After several readings, pause before the rhyming words, and let your child chime in.

Now let's read *Bats*. If your child is a beginning reader, have him or her first read it silently. Then ask your child to read it aloud. For children who are not yet reading, read the book aloud as you run your finger under the words. Ask your child to imitate, or "echo," what he or she has just heard.

Discussing the book's content with your child:
Explain to your child that bats are mammals because their babies are born live; they do not hatch from eggs. Also, the babies (called pups) get milk from their mothers.

At the back of the book is a fun Hop Scotch game. Your child will take pride in demonstrating his or her mastery of the phonic sounds and the high-frequency words.

Enjoy Compass Point Phonics Readers and watch your child read and learn!

Flying Man

Flying-man, **Flying**-man,
Up in the **sky,**
Where are you going to,
Flying so **high?**

Over the mountains,
And over the sea,
Flying-man, **Flying**-man,
Can't you take me?

A bat is a mammal.
It is the only mammal that can fly.
A bat can fly high in the sky.
It can fly fast, too.

Bats are not all the same size.

Bats may be big.

Bats may be small.

One kind of bat is small as a bee!

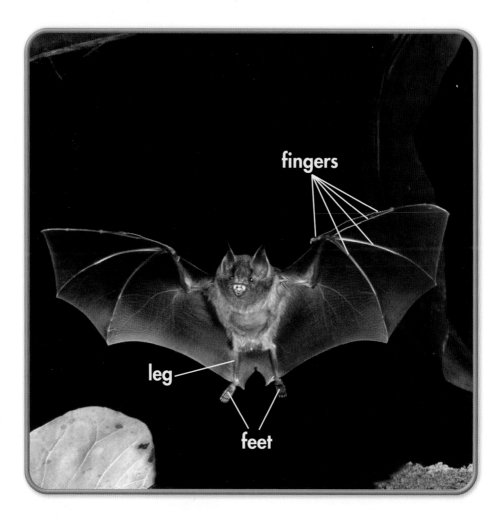

fingers

leg

feet

A bat has fur.
A bat has two legs and two feet.
A bat has ten fingers, too.
What can you find here?

Many bats live in caves
far from the light.
Bats sleep in the daytime.
They sleep upside down.

Bats can see well in the dark.
They hunt for food at night.
When you are asleep, a bat
wakes up.

Some bats eat fruit.
The bats drop the seeds as they fly.
The seeds land on the soil.
New fruit trees will grow.

Some bats eat bugs.
A bat can eat 600 bugs in 1 hour!
Those bugs will not bug you.
So, you see, bats help us a lot.

Word List

Long *i (i, igh, y)*

i
find
kind

igh
high
light
night

y
fly
sky

Homophones
be, bee
too, two

High-Frequency
here
only

Science
fingers
fur
hour
mammal

Hop Scotch

You will need:
- 1 penny
- 2 moving pieces, such as nickels or checkers

Player 1

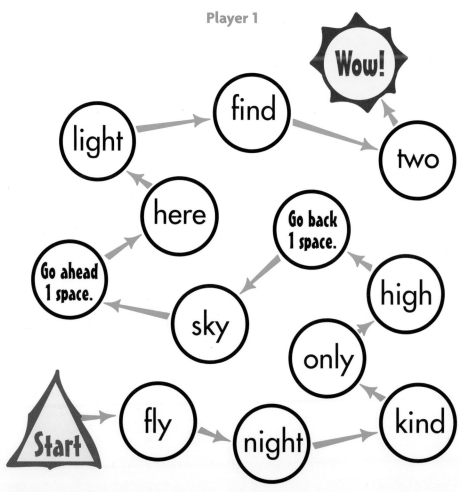

14

How to Play

- Each player puts a moving piece on his or her Start. Players take turns shaking the penny and dropping it on the table. Heads means move 1 space. Tails means move 2 spaces.
- The player moves and reads the word in the circle. If the child cannot read the word, tell him or her what it is. On the next turn, the child must read the word before moving.
- If a player lands on a circle having special directions, he or she should move accordingly.
- The first player to reach the *Wow!* sign wins the game.

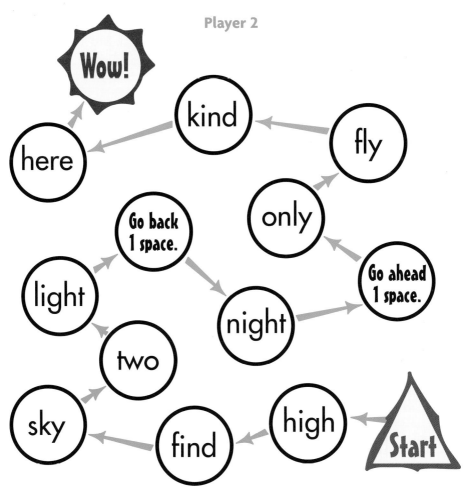

Player 2

Read More

Delafosse, Claude. *Caves.* Hidden World Series. New York: Scholastic, 2000.

Schaefer, Lola M. *What Is a Mammal?* Mankato, Minn.: Pebble Books, 2001.

Theodorou, Rod. *Gray Bat.* Animals in Danger Series. Chicago, Ill.: Heinemann Library, 2001.

Whitehouse, Patricia. *Bats.* What's Awake? Series. Chicago, Ill.: Heinemann Library, 2003.

Index